The 1 Week Minimalist Challenge

Become A Minimalist In A Week And Feel The Positive Effects

Table of Contents

Introduction

This book contains proven steps and strategies on how to apply the principles of minimalism in different aspects of your life, so you can have more time, space, energy and money for what truly makes you happy. You no longer need to feel enslaved by the culture of excess that compels you to crave more and more. If you look into your own life, you can see just how much the unnecessary materials and activities burden your life. They become obstacles between you and a truly fulfilling life. Now you can let go of all those burdens and start to become a true minimalist.

Day 1: Understanding The Fundamentals Of Minimalism

What is a minimalist life?

Minimalism is a lifestyle choice devoid of material excess, so you can have enough space for items that give you true joy. It is the elimination of clutter to help you feel light, free and at peace. As a minimalist, you do not crave for more. You have no urge to always acquire, consume and shop. You do not believe that bigger is necessarily better. You free yourself from the burden of owning physical goods.

As a minimalist, you embrace the beauty in having less. You appreciate the appeal of sparseness. You find contentment from having just what you need and what truly makes you happy.

The acquisition of physical things does not make you particularly happy. In fact, aiming to earn more and have more feels empty and meaningless. You realize that feeling constantly busy, frantic, and anxious is actually quite undesirable.

You feel deep satisfaction waking in the morning to a clutter-free room. You enjoy doing the activities that make you feel alive instead of tolerating work only to fund all the new material items you think you need. You enjoy your life and not your stuff. You do not crave travel, parties and other expensive modes of entertainment to be happy. You have figured out what makes you truly happy and gotten rid of the other things that add no value to your life. Your life is not a life of emptiness or boredom. Your life is full even though you have less. The life of one minimalist is different from the life of another. Each one has to discover what truly makes him or her happiest and creates a life accordingly. Through the following chapters, you can find that specific path for you.

Basic Minimalist Principles

Being a minimalist does not only mean owning fewer belongings. You also need to understand that minimalism is not an end in and of itself. Minimalism is a path toward gaining more freedom, time, and space for the important parts of life. Through minimalism, you can have fewer worries and more pleasure. Minimalism asks you to become more frugal, so you can live a healthier and greener lifestyle.

Some of the fundamental minimalist principles you need to fully understand are as follows:

- Get rid of your unnecessary things. The operative word here is "unnecessary." Being a minimalist does not mean you live a life of deprivation. Rather, you are only supposed to live with what you truly need.

- Determine what is truly essential to you. Which possessions have the greatest importance to you? Which specific things actually make you happy? Which particular items have the biggest effect on your life and on your career?

- Make everything you own count. Make the conscious decision about every possession you plan to keep in your life and whatever activities you plan to do. Every item and activity should be worth your time.

- Fill up your life with joy. Being a minimalist does not mean you simply empty out your life. It means you make space for the wonderful things that can truly make you happy.

- Revise, revise, and revise. Again, minimalism is not an end in itself. Brace yourself for a continuous process of revisiting, revising and adjusting.

In everything you do, always try to determine how you can apply these fundamental principles. Do not become too obsessive about it, but take the time to examine the things that you do, how you do them, and whether or not they are fully necessary.

How You Can Become a Minimalist

The principles of minimalism appeal to many people. You can easily read many things about minimalism on the internet, but appreciating the principles of minimalism is much easier than living it.

A lot of people strive to live by the principles of minimalism, but they often have no idea where to start. There are many changes that must be made to start living the principles of minimalism, and it is common to feel overwhelmed. However, the following guidelines should help point you in the right direction to start becoming a minimalist:

1. Begin by recognizing that you already have more than enough. This is an important step.

To become a true minimalist, you need to become contented with what you already have. If you cannot internalize this idea, all the future de-cluttering activities you do will be for naught because deep inside, you still want to have more.

2. Begin eliminating your clutter and excess possessions. A simple way to find out if you already practice minimalism is to take a look at your home and office. If there is a lot of clutter, you still have a long way to go. You can choose between spending a couple of weekends to clear out all your clutter or spreading the task over a longer period. The decision is yours, but whatever you choose, you must commit.

3. Begin streamlining your schedule. Start cutting back on your commitments and taking the non-essential activities from your schedule. Upon adopting this practice, you can concentrate on what is truly important because you have the space and time to.

4. Gradually revise everything you do. As you make the principles of minimalism an integral part of your life, prepare yourself to revise everything you do in a gradual manner.

Learn How to Be Content

This is the first step to take before proceeding with minimalism. It is not adequate to simply strip everything bare because you will eventually acquire new clutter. To prevent this, you need an attitude change. Understand that the root of your desire for more possessions is your discontent with how things are right now.

If you continue purchasing items you do not need, one possible reason is that you have dissatisfaction in one or more areas of your life. You are not satisfied with the things you currently have, so you try to ease the discontent with new, exciting materials. You desire for more fun, excitements and new ways to make your life happier and more fulfilling. You desire new things that appear cooler than what you own now. Whatever your real reasons are, the truth is that you are not truly happy with what you currently have.

This is a serious problem but know that the solution to the problem does not have to be complex. Here are some useful techniques on learning to be content:

- Know that you already have everything you truly need. What do we truly need? Food to eat, water to drink, shelter and basic clothing to protect us, and family and friends to love and to love us. All other things are extra. You do not actually need all of those state-of-the-art gadgets. You do not need name brand clothes and shoes. You do not need a big house and fancy car.

- Stop purchasing non-essentials. This may really sound hard to do, but the trick is to stay aware of it. One effective method is to begin your own 30-day list. Stick to the rule that if you feel the urge to purchase a non-essential item, write it on your 30-day list first. Make sure that you also write down the date when you added the item on the list. The second part of the rule is that you must not purchase that item for a minimum of 30 days. If you still have the desire to buy the item even after the 30-day waiting time, go ahead and buy it. This method has worked for a lot of people because their desire to buy often evaporates. Before buying anything, ask yourself if the item is truly necessary.

- Be happy by doing, not owning. One great way to start being happy with only the true essentials is to learn that owning material things is not what makes you happy. Rather, what you do truly makes you happy – talk with your friends, take a walk in the park with your kids, cook, sing, jog, create something, or work on a project that truly excites you. If you learn how to concentrate on activities that make you happy, you will realize that you need fewer belongings.

- Discover the idea of "Enough." You do not always need more. After you have reached a particular point, you already have enough. The secret is in learning how to identify that exact point. Normally, people fail to realize they have enough and become absorbed in the cycle of wanting more.

Having more stuff triggers wanting more, and it can be a vicious cycle. You can even become addicted to owning and acquiring. You need to discover when enough is enough and start being happy with all the things you already have. This change does not come about overnight, so go easy on yourself. It will take some time to absorb this concept fully. However, what you need to do now is start being conscious of the concept. Be aware of what you truly need, of what you only want, of wanting more, of being content, and of finding happiness in doing and not in owning. In time, this awareness will lead to a contentedness with the things you already own. This is the groundwork for a minimalist lifestyle.

Simplify What You Do

Becoming a minimalist not only means you start getting rid of physical clutter in your life. It is actually about moderating the clutter of your work life, your demanding schedule, and all the running around that you may be accustomed to. Being a minimalist means you only do what is truly necessary, so you have more time to do what makes you happy.

The vital step to can take in simplifying your schedule is to list all of your commitments and choose which ones are the most essential. By commitment, I mean all of the tasks that eat up your time. This includes your projects at work, any side jobs you may be doing, and the time you spend doing civic work. It includes the time you spend in fixing up your house and attending meetings at your kids' school.

It can sometimes be very easy to agree to commitments presented to us by other people. Before you know it, these commitments have already taken over your life and you have little or no time left to do the things that are truly important to you. Being a minimalist, you need to limit your commitments to include only the most essential so you can avoid burnout and have enough space for what you love.

You can accomplish this by making a list of all the commitments you can think of. Include all the things you do regularly and all the appointments you have committed to both in the short and long term.

After you have completed your list of commitments, choose only four or five that you deem most important. These commitments involve things that you value most. These commitments should be on the top of your priorities list. You should then proceed to removing all the other commitments, as much as possible. You can remove these unnecessary commitments by making phone calls or sending emails to inform people that you are no longer able to commit to what you originally agreed on. Yes, I know how hard and uncomfortable this can be because saying "no" and disappointing others can be difficult. However, know this one important thing: they will live. They will carry on with their lives. Do not be afraid of disappointing other people because it is seldom as bad as you fear.

The process of removal is also a gradual one. There are certain commitments you can remove from your life instantly, but other may take some time. Just remember that your goal is to remove all unnecessary commitments in your schedule eventually. You can do it. You can gradually remove these commitments either by learning how to say "no" or by letting them end naturally.

Day 2: Creating A Minimalist Home

A minimalist's home is not entirely bare or empty. Instead, it is relatively free of clutter. It only has the essential furniture and fixtures. Various knick-knacks do not clutter the counters and tabletops. However, having a minimalist home does not mean you should make your house lacking in fun, character and life. The opposite is actually true. When you have an uncluttered home, you can enjoy the things that truly make you happy – the things that give your life fun, excitement and inspiration to do the activities that give you fulfillment.

Here are just some of the benefits you can get from having a minimalist home:

- You will feel less stressed. You can consider clutter a kind of visual distraction. When your home is too crowded, your attention gets pulled toward the clutter instead of the things that can make you feel calm, relaxed and inspired. When you maintain an uncluttered house, you reduce the visual stress inside your home.

- A minimalist home also looks more charming and appealing. Imagine the pictures of homes in the magazine and how the most appealing are those with hardly anything in them except for some attractive furniture, some pieces of beautiful artwork, and very limited lovely ornaments.

- The most important benefit of a minimalist home is that it is easier to clean. Dusting and cleaning a lot of knick-knacks or sweeping or vacuuming around a lot of furniture can be tedious. The more things you store inside your house, the more time and effort you need to keep them clean and tidy.

How Your Minimalist Home Should Look

As mentioned in the previous chapter, homes of minimalists do not all look the same. They are all different depending on the tastes of the minimalists and how intense a minimalist they choose to become. Just so you have an idea though, here are the common features of a minimalist home:

- A minimalist house, of course, has limited furniture. It only contains a small number of basic furniture pieces. For instance, in the bedroom, you only find a simple bed, a bureau and a bookshelf or nightstand.

- You should see many clear surfaces. Not including a couple of accent decorations, all the flat surfaces in the rooms are clear of knick-knacks and other clutter. You will not see heaps of papers and books lying around.

- We can all agree that making your home totally barren would be quite boring. Therefore, rather than placing a completely empty coffee table in your living room, you can add a basic vase with a couple of flowers. Alternatively, you can add a simple picture frame with your family photo on your work desk. You can also add classy artwork on your wall to create personality and life.

- Always keep this mantra in mind: quality over quantity. Rather than having 20 or more items in your room, you can opt to own a handful of quality things that you truly love and that you use frequently. Choose to have a truly fine table instead of buying five pieces of low quality furniture.

How to Start Creating Your Own Minimalist Home

1. Work with one room at a time. Working with the whole house at once can be a difficult endeavor. To avoid becoming overwhelmed, concentrate on just one room and allow that room to become your center of calm. Then, you can use that simplified room as your inspiration for working on the next room.

2. Survey your furniture, as furniture often takes up the most space. Inspecting what furniture to let go of is the best way to start streamlining your house. As long as you keep things within reason, you can start eliminating as much furniture as you can. Determine the furniture you can discard without depriving your house of comfort and livability. It is ideal to stick to a couple of pieces of furniture that are simple with subdued, solid colors.

3. Always stick to the essentials only. You need to keep this in mind whether you are inspecting your furniture or other things inside your house. You always need to ask the question: Can you live without this particular thing? If the answer to this question is "yes", you can decide to let go of that thing. Remember, your goal is to strip down your house to its essentials. Do not worry. You can

simply add a couple of special and worthy items to your bare necessities after you have simplified your house.

4. The floor should be entirely empty except for the essential pieces of furniture. Make sure that there is not clutter on the floor. Do not leave anything stacked and stored on the floors in your house. After you have chosen the essential furniture you will keep, let go of everything else by donating it, throwing it in the trash or finding storage for it out of view.

5. Stow away things you do not want to let go, but make sure they are out of sight. As mentioned in the previous step, everything you need to keep should be stored in a place hidden from view such as cabinets and drawers. You can install a bookshelf in your room to store CDs, DVDs or books, but make sure that you do not store other things there, especially your knick knacks.

6. To prevent your rooms from looking lifeless and boring, you can opt to place simple photos, drawings or paintings on the walls. Make sure you use frames with subtle and solid colors. However, as much as possible, try to leave some of the walls bare.

7. You can also opt to have a couple of simple decorations to function as accents to your minimalist rooms. The most common examples are plants in small pots or fresh flowers in simple vases. If you are using subtle colors for the rest of your house, you can have simple decorations or accents in bright colors like yellow or red. The bright

colors attract attention and provide your simple room with a dash of energy.

8. Know how to use solid colors and plain patterns. Solid colors are ideal for furniture and floor coverings (if you choose to have them). Avoid using checkered and floral patterns because they can create visual clutter in your rooms. Aside from the dash of colors from your accents, you should try to use subdued colors in your house. White is the classic color used by minimalists, but you do not need to stick with white if you do not like it. You can use any solid color you prefer, as long as it is not stressful to the eyes. Good options include earth colors: tans, browns, greens and blues.

9. Revise and continue purging. After you have started simplifying your rooms, you can still do more simplifying. After the day is done, focus on simplifying the other areas of your life, and then go back and inspect your rooms again after a couple of days with a fresh eye. Is there anything else you can let go? Can you store some of the remaining things away from view? Do you still have something not truly essential? Do this every couple of months, and you will surely find something to eliminate. You will be surprised that you can take your already minimalist home one step further.

10. Another important step to take is determining a place for everything and making sure you remember where those places are. Where will you put your kitchen equipment – your coffeemaker, blender and toaster? Give each

item its own spot, and stick to those spots. Try to find the most logical place to put your items to help maintain your home more easily.

11. After you have done the initial simplification of your house, do not forget to sit back and take pleasure in your accomplishment. Spend a few moments to relish how serene and gratifying your house has become. That is your reward for all the effort you have made.

Day 3: Discover Minimalist Food

Most experts agree that we are eating way too much, especially when compared to our forefathers. With the growing number of overweight and obese people, the motivation to eat less has become more popular. People have become aware that the secret to a healthier lifestyle does not lie with fad diets and non-fat and sugar-free foods but on eating less. However, eating less can be more difficult than it sounds.

Do realize one thing, though. When it comes to food, minimalism is about more than eating less. It involves the actual food you eat and the methods you use in preparing them. It is ideal to eat foods in the most natural state you can find them in. Stay away from processed foods as much as possible. Also try to use simple food preparation methods, so you spend less time in the kitchen.

How to Eat Less

If you are overweight or on your way to being so and you suddenly chose to eat less, it will actually solve many of your health issues. It is important for you to eat the right kinds of food and to exercise regularly, but consuming too many calories is a big problem for many overweight and obese people.

When you consume too many calories on a daily basis, over a long period of time, the calories accumulate as fat. The human body actually needs a little fat to function properly, but excessive fat can cause all sorts of health issues.

Here are some techniques on how you can consume fewer calories:

- Eat until you are nearly full. Do you know that the Okinawans are some of the healthiest people in the world? They will only eat until their stomachs are around 80 percent full. Follow their example, and stop eating once your hunger pangs subside.

- Make sure your meals have smaller portions and lighter foods. Stay away from heavy and big meals.

- Consume foods that are rich in fiber and water. Go with vegetables, beans and fruits, which are both healthy and filling.

- Stay away from restaurants and fast food chains that offer meals in huge quantities. You can still go out and dine at restaurants occasionally, but make sure you stick with salads and side dishes. You can also opt to divide a big meal with another person.

- Try fasting for around 18 to 24 hours once or twice per week. This may sound inconsistent with what you normally hear from health experts, but go ahead and read *Eat Stop Eat* written by Brad Pilon to better understand the idea behind the concept.

How to Eat Clean

Consuming fewer calories can solve a lot of health issues, but it can be more effective when you combine it with clean eating. The main objective is to eat food in its natural condition. This means staying away from processed foods as much as possible.

However, eating food in its natural state does not mean you should only eat them raw, even though raw food is better. Rather, a whole food diet with unprocessed foods, a method that is also known as "clean eating," is actually ideal.

Here are some of the foods you can eat when you want to eat "clean:"

- Foods eaten in their most natural condition or closest to it. This means you need to stay away from processed foods.

- Vegetables and fruits are good choices.

- Legumes and nuts, including nut oil and natural nut butter, are also good choices.

- Whole grains. Look for those that have not been ground into flour.

- Lean protein

You do not need to completely eliminate the foods you like from your diet. It is not advisable to eat healthy 100% of the time. You need to allow yourself to enjoy your favorite foods such as chocolate bars, ice cream, beer, soda and pizza once in a while. The ideal target is to eat healthy foods at least 90 percent of the time. Just keep in mind that you need to do things in moderation.

Cooking Simply

It is always ideal to cook for yourself. This not only enables you to save more money, but you can eat more healthily, as well. There is no doubt about the convenience you get from dining in restaurants, but you get that convenience in exchange for more expensive and unhealthier food choices. While a lot of restaurants are now offering healthy meals, you still get them in big servings, which can actually be unhealthy.

The secret really is in cooking for yourself, but make sure you do the cooking in a simple way. Stick with recipes that are not only simple to prepare but that also require shorter cooking time. Go with ingredients that are natural and simple. There are a lot of excellent spices you can use to add flavor to your dishes without increasing your sugar and fat intake.

The ideal cooking methods include grilling, baking, stir-frying and making soups. As much as possible, try cooking more than what you will eat in one meal, so you can have leftovers for later meals.

Create a Minimalist Kitchen

Aside from clean eating, you also need to maintain a minimalist kitchen. Inspect all the pans, pots, silverware and dishes stored in your kitchen and determine which ones are truly essential. Then, discard all the rest to create more space in your kitchen. Add to that a cutting board and a few sharp knives, and you are good to go. You do not need all those single-use kitchen gadgets and tools such as ice cream scoopers, juice makers and waffle irons. They only eat up space, and you hardly use them. Give them away to your family and friends who need them more.

Do you need to adopt veganism?

No. You do not have to be a vegetarian or a vegan to live a minimalist lifestyle. However, the concepts of veganism and vegetarianism are closely related to minimalism because both concepts require you to use as few resources as you can. Extreme vegan minimalists only consume food they deem necessary. Since dairy, egg and meat are deemed unnecessary in a healthy lifestyle (yes, they are considered a luxury), vegans do without them. In addition, vegans consider eating meat and dairy as immoral.

If you ever wish to explore becoming a vegan or a vegetarian, you do not have to go through a difficult transition. You do not even need to do the transition instantaneously. It is better to shift to a new diet in a slow and gradual manner, so it becomes more manageable and sustainable. Try to gradually increase the amount of vegetarian dishes in your everyday meals by dropping one type of meat or animal product at a time. Eventually, your system becomes accustomed to the new diet.

Many people consider becoming a vegan as beneficial as becoming a minimalist. A lot of people do not realize that they have become unconsciously drawn to eating meat and other animal food products because of the barrage of advertisements we see and hear.

Day 4: Get Into A Minimalist Fitness Regime

Getting into a fitness regime is a difficult task for many people. A lot of them either hate any physical activity or postpone it for a number of different reasons. However, getting into a fitness regime does not need to be complicated or hard. What is the minimum amount of physical exercises you need to become and stay fit? Which particular kinds of physical exercise do you have to perform? What specific kinds of equipment do you need to have?

With minimalist fitness, your focus will be on working out less compared to what other routines require you to do – and with less equipment. The two most common excuses given by people who fail to exercise are lack of time and lack of money required by a fitness regime.

Less Time

You do not need to spend one to two hours in the gym every day to stay fit. If you exercise properly, you can manage with only one to two hours per week. Actually, if you are just beginning a new exercise routine, it is ideal to begin small and slowly. If you have been inactive for a long time, walking for 15 to 20 minutes a couple of times per week is a good start. If you are already active, you can walk for 20 minutes every day at least five times per week. In time, you can increase the duration to 30 minutes, but 20 minutes is already enough to get adequate exercise.

Can you really not spare 15 to 20 minutes of your time every day to save your own life? You can choose to do it in the morning right after you wake up, or you can do it at lunch or after you are done with work. You can even do it on your way home.

If you have already been active for a couple of months, you can start doing interval workouts (walk/run or jog/run or slow/fast biking or swimming). You can also start introducing bodyweight workouts into your fitness regime. The secret is in getting active most days of the week. Ideally, you should work out four to five times per week. Just push yourself to get out of the house. Do something you really enjoy. If you want, you can play basketball, jump rope with your children, go skating, play rugby or soccer, surf, paddle, hike or climb mountains.

If you find yourself going longer than 20 to 30 minutes because you are enjoying it, that is definitely okay. Nevertheless, always remember that it is not necessary.

Minimal Fitness Equipment

You do not need any equipment to become fit and to have great workouts. With only a couple of simple items, you can transform those great workouts into fantastic ones. Moreover, because you need little or no equipment to have a fantastic workout, you can perform it in the comfort of your home or any place you might be. You will find it difficult to give the excuse that you have no time for this kind of workout – you can even finish it while you watch your favorite show on TV.

You can use your own bodyweight to perform a host of challenging exercises. You just need to design a workout you can do even when you cannot go to the gym. There is a lot of simple equipment you can easily buy to make your workouts more interesting and this includes medicine balls, kettle bells, jump ropes and chin-up bars. These tools enable you to easily up the challenge of your workouts.

However, using just your bodyweight is ideal since you do not have to pay for any gym memberships or costly workout equipment. You can also choose to workout anytime and anywhere since most of the exercises include many of your muscles working in coordination. This can then result in improved strength and better overall fitness. If you are just beginning your strength training program, bodyweight is normally more than enough to start with. In addition, it can provide you with a solid foundation of strength you can enhance father later on.

It is highly recommended to start with bodyweight exercises and simply transition to a combination of weight and bodyweight training at a gradual pace. The combination of weight and bodyweight will provide you a good balance during your workouts. This means that even if you have already become strong enough to perform total weight training programs, it is still ideal to utilize bodyweight exercises during those times that you cannot go the gym.

Here is a simple bodyweight workout you can try: a circuit of chin-ups, pull-ups, planks, pushups, diamond pushups, jump squats and hanging knee raises. You do not need to stick to this workout because there are many other bodyweight routines you can choose from. It is ideal to mix them up with various cardiovascular exercises, too.

Make it your habit to get out of the house and stay active. Ride a bike, take a walk or jog, if you wish. Use a jump rope, a dumbbell, a kettle bell or barbell. You can even do martial arts, if you like. As you become more fit, try making your workouts shorter but more intense.

Day 5: Simplify Your Wardrobe And Grooming Routine

Creating a minimalist wardrobe can really be a great challenge for a lot of people. This can even become a greater challenge when you add creating a minimalist grooming routine into the picture. It is very common to see people with big dressers and closets that overflow with garments and clothes. Some people even forgot about the clothes they stored in their closets. Not only is it overwhelming to have too many clothes, it can also be uneconomical.

Grooming routines, especially of women, can take longer than one hour and this is true even if they are in a rush. Like them, you probably have various cabinets and drawers filled with grooming items from hair accessories to makeup to different lotions for the different parts of your body to razors, tweezers, nail kits and scissors and to different products for your hair, teeth, face. You can have all sorts of soaps and body wash, hair shampoo, hair conditioner, facial wash and lots more.

If you find it hard to stick to a minimal grooming products and routine, you may need to reconsider your needs. So, where do you start? Start with this thought: you do not really need all the things you think you need. Just think of the people who reside in Third World countries. A lot of them are not able to use any grooming products at all. Thus, you have more than you really need. The trick is in finding the right balance, so you can live a comfortable life without becoming excessive.

Minimalist Wardrobe

The secret to owning a functional wardrobe without having closets overflowing with clothes is to have various alternatives that can all go well together. All the tops and shirts you own should go well with all the shorts, pants and skirts you have. You can achieve this by choosing a specific style and a specific color scheme for your wardrobe. For instance, you can opt to go with clothes that are in plain and solid blacks, blues, browns, tans, greens and greys. Of course, this should not stop you from choosing bright colors if that is what you prefer. The trick is to find a specific color scheme that you like.

Buy clothes that have classic styles, so they will not easily get outdated. Instead of buying 30 pieces of cheap clothes, buy fewer pieces with high quality. You end up saving more because your clothes do not start falling apart after only a few of washes. It can definitely feel great to have loads of clothes, but you need to learn how to let go of your desire them. You will feel better if you have quality clothes that you can cherish longer.

Go over all the clothes in your closets and drawers by taking all of them out and separating them into two stacks: clothes you have actually worn in the previous six months and clothes that you have not worn recently. Obviously, if the clothes are seasonal, like winter coats, you need to give them a twelve-month timeline. Place the recently worn clothes back inside your closet. The clothes you have not been wearing recently, you can either donate them to your preferred charity or give them to friends and family who can still use them.

After you have sorted your clothes, commit to avoid shopping for new clothes as much as possible. Tell yourself you will only shop for new clothes or shoes when the need is absolute. Even when you think it is extremely necessary, consider buying from a second-hand store. If you feel the temptation to shop, always ask this question: "Will I really use this regularly?" If your answer is "no" or "I am not sure," then do not purchase it.

Grooming

Minimalist grooming can be quite a tough matter, particularly for women. It is rather difficult to give expert advice on how women should groom themselves, especially since different skin types require different care routines. However, you should still make it a point to minimize the amount of grooming aids you use as much as possible. Every time you are tempted to buy fancy hair conditioners you see in TV ads, ask yourself if you truly need it.

Keep your hair as low-maintenance as possible, so you do not need a ton of hair products or time for styling it. Again, the rule is to keep everything simple. If you keep your grooming routine simple, you waste less of time in front of a mirror. You can actually use your time for more productive tasks.

Day 6: Create A Minimalist Workspace

How cluttered is your workspace? If it is overflowing with piles of papers, small gadgets and knick-knacks, you have not yet experienced the joy of working in an uncluttered workspace. There is no standard for a minimalist workspace – it depends on the person using it. For some extreme minimalists, their workspace consists of nothing else but themselves. No piles of papers, no computer, and sometimes there is not even a desk. They work, think and sit on the floor. Obviously, this workspace setup is not for everyone. What you need to do is determine the minimum requirements for your job and concentrate on building a workspace that delivers these essentials and nothing else. Look for ways to streamline and optimize your work processes. Then, determine the tools and equipment you need to accomplish your workflow effectively and efficiently. Get rid of anything that will not contribute to your productivity.

How will you determine your requirements?

You may be surprised to realize that the things you think are necessary may actually be non-essentials. More often than not, we are so accustomed to using our gadgets that we tend to think we absolutely need them. Have you ever wondered if you need all those papers and sticky notes? How much more effective do you really become with all those office tools – 5 pens, 10 pencils, 3 notebooks, calendars, personal organizers, notepads, hole puncher, stapler, and so much more? The objective here is for you to find ways to optimize your work methods, so you can finish your work as effectively as you can without needing all your tools and gadgets.

We all have different requirements, so no one method exists to create a minimalist workspace. However, there are general tips you can use to build your own minimalist workspace. You may realize that not all of the techniques discussed below are applicable to you, so simply choose the techniques you think will make your work processes more efficient.

1. Try working with only one inbox. If you cannot eliminate papers entirely in your work processes, you can try keeping only one inbox tray on your work desk. The trick is to make sure that all the papers that go through you, including telephone messages and post-its, go into that inbox tray. When you implement this, you may have to inform your colleagues about it, so they do not leave papers anywhere on your work desk. Do not spread your papers on your work desk, except when you are working directly with them. You may also choose to keep a folder for your "working files" where you can store the documents that are in progress but do not require attention at immediately. Just make sure that you keep this folder inside a drawer, so it does not clutter your work desk.

2. Make it a habit to empty your inbox every day. Make sure that no paper goes back into the inbox after you have worked on it. Always keep in mind that it is not a storage box but,

rather, your inbox. In order to empty your inbox easily, process the documents from the top down, and make sure you focus on just one item at a time. Decide on each paper and complete the action required as quickly as you can. You can decide to immediately file it in a separate folder, throw it in the trash, forward it to another colleague, take direct action or include it in your to-do list, or store it in your work-in-progress folder so you can go back to it at a later time.

3. Free your work desk from clutter. Your work desk should not have anything except for your inbox tray, computer, telephone and perhaps a photograph of your family. Do not place your pens, sticky notes, stapler and any paper you do not need on your desk. Empty your work desk as much as you can. If you feel you need to add more items, go ahead, but make sure they are truly essential. You will realize that you work better with an uncluttered work desk.

4. Throw out your knick-knacks. If you are like other people who think that small trinkets and baubles are essentials, you need to rethink your minimalist philosophies. Remember, if it does not help you be productive and efficient, toss it away.

5. Clear your office walls. Some people have all sorts of paraphernalia posted on the walls of their workplace. Again, these unnecessary things can create visual clutter that can ultimately add to your stress level. Take them off of your walls. If you posted a printed reference guide, save it in your computer and

create a hotkey that enables you to pull up the document with a simple keystroke when you need it.

6. Clear the desktop on your computer. Create specific folders for each file saved in your computer, and organize them in your Documents folder. Do not simply save files on your desktop with a promise that you will transfer it to the proper folder later. Do not delay, and do it now.

7. Revisit your paper requirements. You may have become very accustomed to the way you work now. This is the reason why you should make the effort to revisit your work processes to see how you can possibly digitize your paper requirements. Your objective should be to eradicate paper as much as you can. When you are able to do so, you will see how much progress you can make in creating a minimalist work area.

8. Get rid of any tools that are non-essential. Ponder on every tool you keep on your work desk, work space and in your entire office. Why do you need that hole puncher and stapler? Why do you need to have so many pens? Why do you need to have a scanner or a fax machine? Some of the gadgets, tools and equipment in your office may not really be under your full control, but try eliminating the ones you believe are not essential. If you prefer, you can do the elimination one tool at a time.

9. Streamline your filing system. Do you really need to retain hard copies of documents also

stored in your computer or in an online database? If you are worried that your files will be lost, you can set up a backup files in a secured online server. Digital documents are a lot easier to retrieve and organize. If you think you really require the hard copies of documents, file them alphabetically, and immediately file papers as soon as you get them to avoid piles of random documents. Spend an hour or two every couple of months to revisit your files and to discard any files that are no longer necessary.

10. Go over each of your drawers, one at a time, to see if there are non-essentials you can eliminate. Do this by taking out the entire contents of the drawer and eliminating all the things you do not need. Having draws that open easily and contain only necessary items helps create a low-stress work environment. Assign a specific spot for every item you choose to keep, and ensure you return all of the items to their proper places.

11. Clear the floor in your work area. You should not put anything on the floor except for your work desk and chair. Do not keep any boxes and files on the floor.

Day 7: Aim For Minimalist Finances

For many people, their finances make up one of the most complicated aspects of their lives. However, this does not have to be the case. You just need to make a little effort in simplifying your finances and ending the money problems that many people experience. Here are some useful techniques on how to do this:

1. Put an end to your consumerism. This is the primary step and the most vital one. Oftentimes, we find it easy to be caught in the mentality of impulsive purchases and buying to seek pleasure, relieve stress, or find self-worth. We acquire this mentality from many years of exposure to constant advertisements, and for a lot of us, it is too hard to stop. However, it is achievable. You can begin by being more aware of this particular mentality and by reminding yourself that you will stop looking for pleasure in shopping and acquiring material possessions.

   When you feel the desire to go out and shop, stop and take a deep breath. Place whatever item you want to buy in your thirty day list. This means you will not purchase it until thirty days after you have written it on your list. During this time, the desire usually disintegrates. Always think about each purchase you want to make and ask these questions: "Is this item truly necessary? Can I live without this item?" Make it your philosophy to live only with the most necessary things and to attain happiness from actually

35

doing things, from being with other people and from creating instead of from acquiring material possessions and spending money.

2. Start building your emergency fund. Without such a fund, you may never achieve full financial peace of mind, and your financial life will always feel chaotic. You cannot follow the steps below to creating a minimalist financial life if you do not have an emergency fund because each expense that comes up unexpectedly can disrupt your whole plan. The first thing you need to do is to start setting up your emergency fund of at least $500. You can do this by placing around $50 to $100 to the emergency fund every time you get your paycheck. When you reach your $500 target, you can them aim to increase your emergency fund to $1,000 or more.

To be able to allocate extra money to your emergency fund, you may need to give up your avoidable expenses. Take a close look at how you spend your money, including those regular disbursements such as mortgages that you may have forgotten about. After you have accounted for all your expenses, you can then determine which ones you can eliminate. Do you have a monthly magazine subscription? Stop it now. Look at the other services you regularly pay for, and see if you can do away with them. Stop buying new books, and start exploring the public library. Cut your cable subscription, especially when you barely have time for watching TV. Start making your own coffee at home instead of buying cups of coffee from Starbucks every day. Do you really need the big car you own now? Do you really need to stay in such a big home? Start sorting through your storage room and see what you may be able to sell. How many more shoes do you need? Do you actually need to get the latest gadgets and computers? Limit your expensive entertainment to a couple outings every month. You can find good ways to entertain yourself, family and friends at home without spending a lot of money in expensive restaurants and bars. You may be surprised to realize that you can save enough money from your unnecessary expenses to start your emergency fund immediately.

3. Start getting out of debt. This is another step to achieve minimalist finances. Most people would agree that debt payments are not an essential part of your life. They should not even exist in your life. Yet, until all your debts are fully paid, you will always have worries and problems.

   After you have set up your emergency fund of at least $500, use the majority of your extra funds to pay off your debts. Focus on paying one debt at a time until all your debts are fully paid. However, as you pay your debts, continue putting a small amount of money into your emergency fund.

   You can expect that this step of paying your debts to take the longest time, but it is definitely worth all your efforts. Do not worry. You can still do the other steps below immediately even if your debts are not yet fully paid up.

4. Start using cash instead of credit cards. What many people do not realize is that their credit card bills ruin their finances. Credit cards make it too easy to use money you do not actually have. Consequently, you end up paying even more in interest and other fees. Start ditching your credit cards, and consider using cash and debit cards.

   Using cash is better than credit because you can budget your money more effectively. You can stick to your budget, and you always know how much money is in your savings account. You do not need to track your expenses extensively when you use cash because you only need to check inside your wallet to know if you have been spending too much. You can also try the envelope system in monitoring cash expenses. At the start of the month, place your budgeted amounts of cash into individual envelopes for gas, groceries, bills and your other expenses.

5. Start automating your finances. When you do so, you no longer have so many worries when it comes to paying your monthly bills. You can talk to your bank to learn how to set up an automatic transfer of your salary into your checking account and automatic payments for all your regular bills. You can pay some of your bills through automatic deductions from your checking or savings account while others require you to use the online bill payment system of your own bank. You can set it up so that it debits an exact amount for payment every month. Even the transfers to your savings account or to your emergency fund can

be done automatically. You can also talk to your creditors to determine how you can pay them automatically every month. As much as possible, try using bonuses and tax returns to pay for your regular expenses, such as rental, so you do not have to worry about it every month.

Having a substantial emergency fund can also help in making your automatic transfers easier and worry-free. You will not always worry about whether you have sufficient balance in your account for all the automatic payments you have scheduled. You can actually opt to divide your emergency fund into two accounts – a bigger portion can go to your online savings account and the remaining balance can go to your checking account where you make your automatic payments. This enables you to have comfortable protection in case of unexpected glitches or expenses.

To avoid becoming frustrated, you need to realize that it normally takes some time to get all your finances properly automated. What you can begin doing today is to set up your automatic deposits, transfers, deductions and recurring bill payments. This is also a good way for you to start being paperless because you will not have to sort through a lot of mail from the service companies.

Automating your finances does not mean you will no longer be responsible for your accounts. It is still ideal to put a prompt in your calendar for you to verify the balance in your bank accounts at least once every week. This will give you peace of mind knowing that you can easily catch any glitches or errors before they become full-blown problems. Aside from those weekly bank account verifications, you can start forgetting about your finances.

6. Do not buy anything unless you really need it and you have the money to pay for it. After you have completed all the steps discussed above – you are free of debts, you have a substantial emergency fund, and you have automated your finances – there is still a chance of you going back to your old financial troubles if you do not control your purchases. You need to be mindful of all your spending decisions. Do you really need to buy that piece of furniture/appliance/electronic gadget? To answer this, you need to remind yourself of two things: first, you are not supposed to buy anything unless you really need it and second, you are not supposed to buy anything unless you have the money to pay for it. .

Try staying out of debt as much as you can. You do not need to buy a brand new car. You can wait and save enough money to buy a second-hand car. Again: do not buy anything unless you truly need it and unless you have the money to pay for it at hand. If you adhere to these two basic rules, you will not have to worry about your finances ever again.

Conclusion

I hope this book was able to help you learn the strategies and techniques on transforming yourself into a true minimalist.

The next step is to take on the challenge of becoming a minimalist in a week, but you need to always remember that after jumpstarting your minimalist life in one week, becoming a true minimalist requires a lifetime commitment.

Thank you and good luck!

Made in the USA
Las Vegas, NV
23 October 2022

58010619R00024